DEALING WITH
ANGER

BIBLE STUDY

HOPE FOR THE HEART BIBLE STUDIES

June Hunt

ROSE PUBLISHING/ASPIRE PRESS

Peabody, Massachusetts

ROSE PUBLISHING/ASPIRE PRESS

Hope For The Heart Bible Studies
Dealing with Anger Bible Study

Copyright © 2017 Hope For The Heart
All rights reserved.
Published by Aspire Press, an imprint of
Hendrickson Publishers Marketing, LLC
P. O. Box 3473
Peabody, Massachusetts 01961-3473 USA
www.HendricksonRose.com

Get inspiration via email, sign up at
www.aspirepress.com

For more information on Hope For The Heart, visit www.hopefortheheart.org or
call 1-800-488-HOPE (4673).

Printed in the United States of America
010517VP

CONTENTS

About This Bible Study

THANK YOU. Sincerely. Thanks for taking the time and making the effort to invest in the study of God's Word with God's people. The apostle John wrote that he had "no greater joy than to hear that my children are walking in the truth" (3 John 4). At HOPE FOR THE HEART, our joy comes from seeing God use our materials to help His children walk in the truth.

OUR FOUNDATION

God's Word is our sure and steady anchor. We believe the Bible is *inspired* by God (He authored it through human writers), *inerrant* (completely true), *infallible* (totally trustworthy), and the *final authority* on all matters of life and faith. This study will give you *biblical* insight on the topic of anger.

WHAT TO EXPECT IN THIS BIBLE STUDY

The overall flow of this topical Bible study looks at anger from four angles: Definitions, Characteristics, Causes, and Biblical Steps to Solution.

- The **DEFINITIONS** section orients you to the topic by laying the foundation for a broad understanding of anger from a biblical and psychological standpoint. It answers the question: What does it mean?

- The **CHARACTERISTICS** section spotlights various aspects that are often associated with anger, giving a deeper understanding to the topic. It answers the question: What does it look like?

- The CAUSES section identifies the physical, emotional, and spiritual sources of anger. It answers the question: What causes it?

- The BIBLICAL STEPS TO SOLUTION sections provide action plans designed to help you—and help you help others—deal with anger from a scriptural point of view. It answers the question: What can you do about it?

The individual sessions contain narrative, biblical teaching, and discussion questions for group interaction and personal application. We sought to strike a balance between engaging content, biblical truth, and practical application.

GUIDELINES

Applying the following biblical principles will help you get the most out of this Bible-based study as you seek to live a life pleasing to the Lord.

- PRAY – "Unless the LORD builds the house, the builders labor in vain" (Psalm 127:1). Any progress in spiritual growth comes from the Lord's helping hand, so soak your study in prayer. We need to depend on God's wisdom to study, think, and apply His Word to our lives.

- PREPARE – Even ants prepare and gather food in the harvest (Proverbs 6:6–8). As with most activities in life, you will get out of it as much as you put into it. You will reap what you sow (Galatians 6:7). Realize, the more you prepare, the more fruit you produce.

- PARTICIPATE – Change takes place in the context of community. Come to each session ready to ask questions, engage with others, and seek God's help. And "do everything in love" (1 Corinthians 16:14).

- PRACTICE – James says, "Do not merely listen to the word, and so deceive yourselves. Do what it says" (James 1:22). Ultimately, this Bible study is designed to impact your life.

- **PASS IT ON!** – The Bible describes a spiritual leader who "set his heart to study the Law of the LORD, and to do it and to teach his statutes and rules" (Ezra 7:10 ESV). Notice the progression: *study . . . do . . . teach.* That progression is what we want for your journey. We pray that God will use the biblical truths contained in this material to change your life and then to help you help others! In this way, the Lord's work will lead to more and more changed lives.

OUR PRAYER

At HOPE FOR THE HEART, we pray that the biblical truths within these pages will give you the hope and help you need to handle the challenges in your life. And we pray that God will reveal Himself and His will to you through this study of Scripture to make you more like Jesus. Finally, we pray that God's Spirit will strengthen you, guide you, comfort you, and equip you to live a life that honors Jesus Christ.

A Note to Group Leaders

"Do your best to present yourself to God as one approved, a worker who does not need to be ashamed and who correctly handles the word of truth."

2 Timothy 2:15

Thank you for leading this group. Your care and commitment to the members doesn't go unnoticed by God. Through this study, God will use you to do His work: to comfort, to encourage, to challenge, and even to bring people to saving faith in Christ. For your reference, we've included a gospel message on page 12 to assist you in bringing people to Christ. The following are some helpful tips for leading the sessions.

TIPS FOR LEADERS

* **Pray** – Ask God to guide you, the members, and your time together as a group. Invite the group members to share prayer requests each week.

* **Prepare** – Look over the sessions before you lead. Familiarize yourself with the content and find specific points of emphasis for your group.

* **Care** – Show the members you are interested in their lives, their opinions, and their struggles. People will be more willing to share if you show them you care.

* **Listen** – Listen to the Lord's leading and the members' responses. Ask follow-up questions. A listening ear is often more meaningful than a good piece of advice.

* **Guide** – You don't have to "teach" the material. Your role is to *facilitate group discussion*: ask questions, clarify confusion, and engage the group members.

BEFORE THE FIRST MEETING

Schedule

- Determine the size of the group. Keep in mind that people tend to share more freely and develop genuine intimacy in smaller groups.

- Pick a time and place that works well for everyone.

- Decide how long each session will run. Sessions shouldn't take more than an hour or hour and a half.

- Gather the group members' contact information. Decide the best method of communicating (phone, text, email, etc.) with them outside of the group meeting.

Set Expectations

- **CONFIDENTIALITY** – Communicate that what is shared in the group needs to stay in the group.

- **RESPECTFULNESS** – Emphasize the importance of respecting each other's opinions, experiences, boundaries, and time.

- **PRAYER** – Decide how you want to handle prayer requests. If you take prayer requests during group time, factor in how much time that will take during the session. It may be more effective to gather requests on note cards during the sessions or have members email them during the week.

AT THE FIRST MEETING

Welcome

- Thank the members of your group for coming.

- Introduce yourself and allow others to introduce themselves.

- Explain the overall structure of study (Definitions, Characteristics, Causes, and Biblical Steps to Solution), including the discussion/application questions.

- Pray for God's wisdom and guidance as you begin this study.

LEADING EACH SESSION

Overview

- Summarize and answer any lingering questions from the previous session.

- Give a broad overview of what will be covered in each session.

How to Encourage Participation

- **PRAY.** Ask God to help the members share openly and honestly about their struggles. Some people may find it overwhelming to share openly with people they may not know very well. Pray for God's direction and that He would help build trust within the group.

- **EXPRESS GRATITUDE AND APPRECIATION.** Thank the members for coming and for their willingness to talk.

- **SPEAK FIRST.** The leader's willingness to share often sets the pace and depth of the group. Therefore, it is important that you, as the leader, begin the first few sessions by sharing from your own experience. This eases the pressure of the other members to be the first to talk. The group members will feel more comfortable sharing as the sessions progress. By the third or fourth session, you can ask others to share first.

- **ASK QUESTIONS.** Most of the questions in the study are open-ended. Avoid yes/no questions. Ask follow-up and clarifying questions so you can understand exactly what the members mean.

- **RESPECT TIME.** Be mindful of the clock and respectful of the members' time. Do your best to start and end on time.

- **RESPECT BOUNDARIES.** Some members share more easily than others. Don't force anyone to share who doesn't want to. Trust takes time to build.

Dealing with Difficulties

- You may not have an answer to every question or issue that arises. That's okay. Simply admit that you don't know and commit to finding an answer.

- Be assertive. Some people are more talkative than others, so it is important to limit the amount of time each person shares so everyone has a chance to speak. You can do this by saying something like: "I know this is a very important topic and I want to make sure everyone has a chance to speak, so I'm going to ask that everyone would please be brief when sharing." If someone tries to dominate the conversation, thank them for sharing, then invite others to speak. You can offer a non-condemning statement such as: "Good, thank you for sharing. Who else would like to share?" Or, "I'd like to make sure everyone has a chance to speak. Who would like to go next?"

- Sometimes people may not know how to answer a question or aren't ready to share their answer. Give the group time to think and process the material. Be okay with silence. Rephrasing the question can also be helpful.

- If someone misses a session, contact that person during the week. Let them know you noticed they weren't there and that you missed them.

WRAPPING UP

- Thank the group for their participation.

- Provide a brief summary of what the next session will cover.

- Encourage them to study the material for the next session during the week.

- Close in prayer. Thank God for the work He is doing in the group and in each person's life.

We are grateful to God for your commitment to lead this group. May God bless you as you guide His people toward the truth—truth that sets us free!

*"If [your gift] is to lead,
do it diligently."*

Romans 12:8

FOUR POINTS OF GOD'S PLAN

The gospel is central to all we do at Hope For The Heart. More than anything, we want you to know the saving love and grace of Jesus Christ. The following shows God's plan of salvation for you!

#1 GOD'S PURPOSE FOR YOU IS SALVATION.

God sent Jesus Christ to earth to express His love for you, save you, forgive your sins, empower you to have victory over sin, and to enable you to live a fulfilled life (John 3:16–17; 10:10).

#2 YOUR PROBLEM IS SIN.

Sin is living independently of God's standard—knowing what is right, but choosing what is wrong (James 4:17). The penalty of sin is spiritual death, eternal separation from God (Isaiah 59:2; Romans 6:23).

#3 GOD'S PROVISION FOR YOU IS THE SAVIOR.

Jesus died on the cross to personally pay the penalty for your sins (Romans 5:8).

#4 YOUR PART IS SURRENDER.

Place your faith in (rely on) Jesus Christ as your personal Lord and Savior and reject your "good works" as a means of earning God's approval (Ephesians 2:8–9). You can tell God that you want to surrender your life to Christ in a simple, heartfelt prayer like this: "God, I want a real relationship with You. Please forgive me for my sins. Jesus, thank You for dying on the cross to pay the penalty for my sins. Come into my life and be my Lord and Savior. In Your holy name I pray. Amen."

WHAT CAN YOU EXPECT NOW?

When you surrender your life to Christ, God empowers you to live a life pleasing to Him (2 Peter 1:3–4). Jesus assures those who believe with these words: "Very truly I tell you, whoever hears my word and believes him who sent me has eternal life and will not be judged but has crossed over from death to life" (John 5:24).

SESSION 1

DEFINITIONS OF ANGER

"'In your anger do not sin':
Do not let the sun go down
while you are still angry."

EPHESIANS 4:26

The day begins like any other day, but ends like no other. On this day, he gives full vent to his anger. As a result, he is running for his life.

He is part of a mistreated minority—grievously persecuted—not for doing something wrong, but for being perceived as a threat. Raised with privilege in the palace of a king, he is spared the heartless treatment inflicted on his kinsmen. But watching the injustice day after day and year after year finally becomes too much for him to bear.

When he sees one of his own people suffering an inhumane beating at the hands of an Egyptian, Moses is filled with rage. He snaps. In an instant, he kills the Egyptian and hides the body in the sand. But his angry, impetuous act is not committed in secret. When news of the murder reaches Pharaoh, Moses fears for his life and flees.

The Fire Within

When you look at the life of Moses, you can see both the power and the problems inherent in anger. Has anger ever clouded your judgment to the point that you reacted rashly and lived to regret it? Ultimately, you have the choice to *act* wisely or to *react* foolishly.

In his lifetime, Moses *did both.* Like him, you too can face the fiery anger within and learn to keep it under control. In doing so, you will demonstrate wisdom because . . .

"Fools give full vent to their rage,
but the wise bring calm in the end."
PROVERBS 29:11

In this session, we'll look at definitions of anger, levels of anger, and unhealthy expressions of anger.

Don't let anger
cloud your judgment.

Write from the Heart

Describe what you think the world and *your* life would be like if everyone (including you) handled their anger in a godly way.

INJUSTICE IGNITES ANGER

Understandably, Moses felt anger over the *unjust* treatment of his Hebrew brothers, but what he did with that anger is what caused all the trouble. Moses allowed his anger to overpower him. Acting on impulse, he committed murder.

Although he was right about the *injustice*, he was wrong in his reaction. His hot-blooded volatility revealed how unprepared he was for the task God planned for him. Consequently, God kept Moses on the backside of a desert for the next 40 years so that he would realize that rescuing his own people in *his own way* would ultimately fail.

Moses needed to learn this vital lesson to become the leader through whom God would accomplish His own will in *His own supernatural way*. Moses tried to earn the Israelites' respect by coming to their rescue. Instead, his murderous rage earned only their disrespect.

"Moses thought that his own people would realize that God was using him to rescue them, but they did not."

ACTS 7:25

The Meaning of Anger

Who hasn't lit a candle and become entranced by the flickering flame? As it dances on the wick, it's a delight to see, but dangerous to touch. No one dares to put a finger into even the tiniest of blazes.

Anger is much like the flame of a candle—it's associated with "heat" of varying degrees. Temperatures are determined by the hues of the flame. But no matter the blues, yellows, oranges, and reds, we all know that it's hot and if we hold on to it, we will get burned!

And so it is with anger: The higher the degree of heat, the more people get hurt—*including you.*

> *"Can a man scoop fire into his lap without his clothes being burned?"*
>
> PROVERBS 6:27

- **Anger** is a strong emotion of irritation or agitation that occurs when a need or expectation is not met.[1]

    "An angry person stirs up conflict, and a hot-tempered person commits many sins" (Proverbs 29:22).

- **Angry** people in the Bible are often described as hot-tempered or quick-tempered.

    "A hot-tempered person stirs up conflict, but the one who is patient calms a quarrel" (Proverbs 15:18).

- **Anger** in the Old Testament is most frequently the Hebrew word *aph*, literally meaning "nose or nostrils," figuratively depicting nostrils flaring with anger. Later, *aph* came to represent the entire face as seen in two ancient Hebrew idioms:[2]

  1. "LONG OF FACE" (or nose), meaning *slow to anger.*
     "The Lord is gracious and compassionate, slow to anger and rich in love" (Psalm 145:8).

  2. "SHORT OF FACE" (or nose), meaning *quick to anger.*
     "A quick-tempered person does foolish things" (Proverbs 14:17).

In the New Testament, the Greek word *orge* originally meant any "natural impulse or desire," but later came to signify "anger as the strongest of all passions." It is often translated as *wrath* because of its powerful, lasting nature.[3]

*"For those who are self-seeking
and who reject the truth and follow evil,
there will be wrath and anger."*

ROMANS 2:8

Write from the Heart

Do you tend to think of God as being more angry or patient? Why?

....

....

....

....

....

The Bible describes God as "slow to anger" in numerous places: Exodus 34:6; Numbers 14:18; Nehemiah 9:17; Psalm 86:15; 103:8; 145:8; Joel 2:13; Jonah 4:2; Nahum 1:3. How do these verses affect your understanding of God?

....

....

....

....

....

....

....

....

The Magnitude of Anger

The next time you light a candle, look at the hues and shades of the flame. Notice the light blue at the center—that's actually the hottest part of the flame. The temperature then diminishes from the inner core to the outer sides, signified by shades of yellow, orange, then red.

Likewise, anger can run the gamut from bright red to a light blue. Anger can lightly singe or severely scorch. It ranges from mild agitation to hot explosions, from controlled irritations to uncontrolled eruptions.

In the Bible, Joseph's brothers displayed the destructive heat of anger.

> *"Simeon and Levi . . .*
> *have killed men in their anger. . . .*
> *Cursed be their anger, so fierce,*
> *and their fury, so cruel!"*
>
> GENESIS 49:5–7

Anger is a wide umbrella word covering many levels of the emotion.[4]

- **Indignation is simmering anger** provoked by something appearing to be unjust or unkind and is often perceived as justified.

  Jesus became indignant when the disciples prevented parents from bringing their children to Him so that He might bless them.

  "When Jesus saw this, he was indignant. He said to them, 'Let the little children come to me, and do not hinder them, for the kingdom of God belongs to such as these'" (Mark 10:14).

- **Wrath is burning anger** accompanied by a desire to avenge. Wrath often moves from the inner emotion of anger to the outer expression of anger.

  Romans 1:18 explains that God expresses His wrath as divine judgment on those who commit willful sin.

  "The wrath of God is being revealed from heaven against all the godlessness and wickedness of people, who suppress the truth by their wickedness" (Romans 1:18).

- **Fury is fiery anger** so fierce that it destroys common sense. The word *fury* suggests a powerful force compelled to harm or destroy.

  Some members of the Sanhedrin were fiercely angry with Peter and the other apostles for proclaiming that Jesus was God.

  "They were furious and wanted to put them to death" (Acts 5:33).

- **Rage is blazing anger** resulting in loss of self-control, often to the extreme of violence and temporary insanity.

  After an outburst of rage, a cry of remorseful regret or disbelief is often expressed—"I can't believe I did that!" Yet those who continue to vent their rage toward others, including toward God, find themselves defeated by their own destructive decisions and ruined relationships.

  "A person's own folly leads to their ruin, yet their heart rages against the LORD" (Proverbs 19:3).

The Misuse of Anger

Periodically, everyone feels the heat of anger, but how you handle the heat determines whether or not you are misusing it. The small flame that lights a cozy campfire, if left unchecked, can just as quickly ignite a fierce forest fire. Conversely, the initial spark of anger that could be used for good, if snuffed out too quickly, can keep anger from accomplishing its designated purpose. If you are wise, you have learned how to handle your anger, and you have learned how to help others handle their anger.[5]

The Bible says . . .

"The wise turn away anger."

PROVERBS 29:8

- **Prolonged anger**—the "simmering stew"—is held in for a long time. This anger is a result of an unforgiving heart toward a past offense and the offender. Unforgiveness left unresolved can result in resentment and bitterness.

  Example: "I'll never forgive the way he talked to me years ago."

  But the Bible says, "See to it that no one falls short of the grace of God and that no bitter root grows up to cause trouble and defile many" (Hebrews 12:15).

- **Pressed-down anger**—the "pressure cooker"—is denied or hidden anger. Usually developing from a fear of facing negative emotions, this kind of anger can create a deceitful heart and lead to untruthfulness with others. Failure to honestly confront and resolve angry feelings can result in self-pity, self-contempt, and self-doubt.

Example: "I never get angry, maybe just a little irritated at times."

But the Bible says, "Get rid of all bitterness, rage and anger, brawling and slander, along with every form of malice" (Ephesians 4:31).

- **Provoked anger**—the "short fuse"—is quick and impatient, instantly irritated or incensed. A testy temper is often expressed using criticism or sarcasm under the guise of teasing.

  Example: "I can't believe you said that! You're so childish!"

  But the Bible says, "Do not be quickly provoked in your spirit, for anger resides in the lap of fools" (Ecclesiastes 7:9).

- **Profuse anger**—the "volatile volcano"—is powerful, destructive, and hard to control. This way of releasing anger is characterized by contempt, violence, and abuse toward others.

  Example: "You fool! If you do that again, you'll wish you'd never been born."

  But the Bible says, "I tell you that anyone who is angry with his brother or sister will be subject to judgment. . . . And anyone who says, 'You fool!' will be in danger of the fire of hell" (Matthew 5:22).

Write from the Heart

Do you typically express your anger or bottle it up? What often results from the way you handle your anger?

....

....

....

....

....

....

....

....

....

....

....

....

....

....

....

....

Discussion/Application Questions

1. Think about our culture today. In what specific ways do you see anger being expressed?

....

....

....

....

2. Anger isn't necessarily bad or evil. Even Jesus—who never sinned—became indignant when children were prevented from coming to Him. Describe a situation where anger would be appropriate and could motivate people to do something good.

....

....

....

....

3. Anger can either drive us to say or do things we later regret, or it can be a catalyst to correct an injustice or stand up for something we deeply believe in. What does your anger typically drive you to do?

....

....

....

....

....

....

4. How does your anger affect your relationship with God? How do you relate to God when you're angry?

....

....

....

....

....

5. As you head into the rest of this study, what are your goals concerning anger? What area of your life or relationships would greatly benefit from handling your anger more appropriately?

....

....

....

....

....

....

Notes

> "Now may the Lord of peace himself give you
> peace at all times and in every way."
> 2 Thessalonians 3:16

CHARACTERISTICS OF ANGER

"Everyone should be quick to listen, slow to speak and slow to become angry, because human anger does not produce the righteousness that God desires."

JAMES 1:19–20

Hurt Ignites Anger

Have you ever been hurt or betrayed by a close friend or family member? It's one thing when an enemy hurts you, but betrayal by a friend deeply wounds the soul. So what do you do when opposition comes from among your own circle, your closest confidants, your trusted few?

One national leader, Moses, knew the hurt of such betrayal. He led wisely, demonstrated courage, and won the confidence of his people.

But his authority was undermined by a subordinate who created so much dissension that he successfully stole the loyalty of 250 others. The people who trusted Moses throughout the years, who knew him best, who should have been most loyal turned against him. In response, Moses did not express his anger by taking personal revenge. He did not react impulsively. Rather, he appealed to the Lord to act on his behalf. "Moses became very angry and said to the LORD, 'Do not accept their offering. I have not . . . wronged any of them'" (Numbers 16:15).

Although justifiably angry, Moses learned how to face the fiery anger within and act wisely rather than react foolishly. He restrained his rage, poured out his heart, and pleaded with the Lord to deal with his offenders. In turn, God took up his cause, destroyed his betrayers, and defended his honor. Moses refused to take revenge, but rather allowed the Lord to be his avenger because God had given this promise: "It is mine to avenge; I will repay" (Deuteronomy 32:35).

In this session, we'll look at what triggers our anger, symptoms of anger, and responses to anger.

Write from the Heart

When Moses became angry, he turned to God and poured out his heart. Do you find it difficult to come to God with your anger? Why?

What Are Your Anger Cues?

When it comes to picturing anger, perhaps the most poignant illustration would be the cragged, gargantuan land formations that sputter with steam and spew molten rock—*the volcano.*

Like anger, before a toxic flow emerges, there is a gurgling beneath the surface, a series of events that create instability and set the stage for an explosive outburst. Scientists have learned how to look for cues that a volcano is about to erupt, including the release of steam and gases, small earthquakes and tremors, and swelling of the volcano's slopes.

Similarly, the human body has a *physical reaction* when it experiences anger. These anger cues can alert you when you begin to feel angry. Discerning your own anger cues can help you avoid trouble. Likewise, being aware of the signs of anger in others can alert you to defend yourself, just like a firefighter defends himself by wearing fire-retardant clothing.

A biblical example of an anger cue is Jonathan's loss of appetite when he was hurt and grieved over his father's (King Saul's) unjust, shameful treatment toward his close friend David. "Jonathan got up from the table in fierce anger . . . he did not eat, because he was grieved at his father's shameful treatment of David" (1 Samuel 20:34).

Discerning your anger cues can help you avoid trouble.

Anger Cues Checklist

Identify your anger cues. Place a check mark (√) beside the following statements that are true of you.

- ○ I have a decreased appetite.
- ○ I have tense muscles.
- ○ I feel unusually hot or cold.
- ○ I have increased perspiration.
- ○ I feel flushed.
- ○ I clench my teeth.
- ○ I clench my fists.
- ○ I experience dry mouth.
- ○ I become silent, shutting down verbally.
- ○ I use loud, rapid, or high-pitched speech.
- ○ I breathe faster and harder than normal.
- ○ I experience an upset, churning stomach.
- ○ I walk hard and fast or pace back and forth.
- ○ I have twitches or anxious behaviors (such as tapping a pencil, shaking a foot).
- ○ I use language that is inappropriate, harsh, or coarse, including gossip and sarcasm.
- ○ I feel my heart racing.

When you identify your anger cues, you are in a better position to quickly identify when you are angry and direct your energy to produce a positive outcome.

Symptoms of Unresolved Anger

A volcanic crater contains toxic gases, a steaming underbelly, and razor-sharp rock fragments. Deep within the heart of unresolved anger, the darkened deposits of a critical spirit—bitterness and depression (among other damaging emotions)—can be found.

When volcanologists excavate and analyze material inside a crater, they work as quickly and efficiently as possible, being aware that the longer they stay, the higher the risk of injury or even death.[6] And so it is with unresolved anger. The longer it's allowed to fume and fester, the more dangerous—and even deadly—it can be for you and those around you.

Prolonged anger can create a root of bitterness and an unforgiving heart. Refusing to face your feelings in a healthy way prolongs *unresolved* anger until it eventually becomes *harbored* anger. Unresolved anger can cause significant physical, emotional, and spiritual problems.

Jesus said . . .

*"I tell you that anyone who is angry
with a brother or sister
will be subject to judgment."*

MATTHEW 5:22

Unresolved anger is known to produce some of the following symptoms:[7]

Physical Symptoms

- Blurred vision
- Headaches
- Heart disease
- High blood pressure
- Insomnia
- Intestinal disorders
- Overeating
- Stomach disorders

Emotional Symptoms

- Anxiety
- Bitterness
- Compulsions
- Depression
- Fear
- Insecurity
- Phobias
- Worry

Spiritual Symptoms

- **Loss of confidence:** feeling insecure about your relationship with God and your ability to respond wisely to difficulties

- **Loss of energy:** lacking strength for your service to God and others

- **Loss of faith:** failing to believe that God is working in your life

- **Loss of freedom:** becoming a prisoner of your emotions and unable to serve God freely

- **Loss of identity:** becoming like the person toward whom you are bitter rather than becoming like Christ

- **Loss of perspective:** allowing your emotions to distort your thinking

- **Loss of sensitivity:** failing to hear the Spirit of God speaking to your heart

- **Loss of purpose:** losing a sense of God's purpose for your life

*Prolonged anger
can create bitterness.*

Write from the Heart

Look over the lists of symptoms again. Which ones stand out to you? How does anger affect you physically, emotionally, and spiritually?

Physically:

....

....

....

....

Emotionally:

....

....

....

....

Spiritually:

....

....

....

....

Do You Act or React?[8]

Scientists are continually developing technology to help them *act* in preparation for a volcanic eruption rather than simply *react* to its deadly blast after the fact.

In recent years, monitoring devices known as "spiders" (because of their spindly legs) have been used to crawl around the interior of craters and measure seismic activity. The creator of the device, Rick LaHusen, a hydrologist at the Cascades Volcano Observatory in Vancouver, Canada, observed: "They can analyze their data in real time and decide what's important and what's not important and prioritize it."[9]

People who choose to act rather than react to anger share some similarities with the analytical spiders—reason rules the day and preparedness can help avert great tragedy.

- When you are angry, does reason rule the day or do tense emotions take over?

- Do you make choices that lead to appropriate actions, or do you have knee-jerk responses that lead to inappropriate reactions?

As you evaluate what happens when you feel angry and try to learn how others perceive you when you are angry, seek God's wisdom and understanding.

*"If you call out for insight
and cry aloud for understanding,
and if you look for it as for silver
and search for it as for hidden treasure,
then you will understand the fear of the* Lord
*and find the knowledge of God.
For the* Lord *gives wisdom;
from his mouth come knowledge
and understanding."*

Proverbs 2:3–6

Appropriate Action	Inappropriate Reaction
Appropriate actions express your thoughts and feelings with restraint, understanding, and concern for the other person's welfare.	Inappropriate reactions express your thoughts and feelings in such a way that stirs up anger in others and produces strife.
"The one who has knowledge uses words with restraint, and whoever has understanding is even-tempered." Proverbs 17:27	"As churning cream produces butter, and as twisting the nose produces blood, so stirring up anger produces strife." Proverbs 30:33

Assess how you respond to anger. Do your responses demonstrate appropriate, prepared actions or do your responses demonstrate inappropriate, explosive reactions? Answer the following statements by placing a check mark (√) beside those that are true of you.

When I am angry, I . . .

APPROPRIATE ACTIONS (*Act*)	INAPPROPRIATE REACTIONS (*React*)
○ Use tactful, compassionate words.	○ Use tactless, condemning words.
○ Can see the other person's point of view.	○ See only my point of view.
○ Want to help the one who angers me.	○ Want to punish the one who angers me.
○ Focus on my own faults.	○ Focus only on the faults of others.
○ Have realistic expectations.	○ Have unrealistic expectations.
○ Have a flexible and cooperative attitude.	○ Have a rigid and uncooperative attitude.
○ Forgive personal injustices.	○ Harbor unforgiveness about personal injustices.
○ Act in a gracious way, trusting God with the outcome.	○ Manipulate or intimidate to control the outcome.
○ Trust God to exercise justice according to His timing.	○ Insist on justice according to my timing.

Write from the Heart

In what situations or with which individuals are you most likely to display inappropriate angry reactions?

Read James 1:19. If you applied this verse to the situations or individuals you just mentioned, what would happen? What would the benefits be?

Discussion/Application Questions

1. The things we expose ourselves to can affect our mood. Books, radio, television, video games, Internet, and social media impact our lives in positive and negative ways. What are the benefits and dangers of these types of media, as it relates to anger?

....

....

....

....

....

2. Do you tend to express your anger *inwardly* (at yourself; with condemning thoughts, negative self-talk, worrying, withdrawing, etc.) or *outwardly* (at others; with arguing, belittling, gossiping, swearing, etc.)? Why do you think you express your anger in this way? What changes can you make to express your anger more constructively?

....

....

....

....

....

....

3. Unresolved anger can cause significant physical problems over time. How does anger affect you physically? What will happen if you don't change the way you handle your anger? What are some physical changes you can start making in order to better handle your anger?

....

....

....

....

....

....

4. Is there any unresolved anger in your life that needs to be brought before the Lord? Write out a prayer expressing to God what you're experiencing. Also, consider talking with a trusted friend, counselor, or pastor about helping you work through and process any unresolved anger in your life.

....

....

....

....

....

....

Notes

"Now may the Lord of peace himself give you
peace at all times and in every way."
2 Thessalonians 3:16

SESSION 3

CAUSES OF ANGER

"Then the LORD said to Cain,
'Why are you angry?'"

GENESIS 4:6

Fear Ignites Anger

Imagine leading thousands of people through the desert with all of them looking to you to meet both their physical and spiritual needs. While setting up camp at the base of a mountain, God calls you to climb the mountain and meet with Him because He plans to give you the Ten Commandments and other beneficial laws.

As you meet with God, unbeknownst to you, the very people God has instructed you to lead have turned their hearts away from Him. They melt their precious gold, mold a golden calf, and worship it! Now, God interrupts your meeting to inform you that your people have turned against Him. Flushed with anger and fear, you rush down the mountain to confront them.

Exodus 32:19 states, "When Moses approached the camp and saw the calf and the dancing, his anger burned and he threw the tablets out of his hands, breaking them to pieces at the foot of the mountain."

Anger is often associated with other emotions. Moses reacted in anger because he was full of fear. He was afraid God's righteous anger against his disobedient people would result in their destruction. Anger is thus a revealing emotion. It can tell you something deeper about what you are feeling or thinking.

Anger is a revealing emotion.

In this session, we'll look at some of the causes and associated feelings and beliefs that often accompany anger.

As we search our hearts and uncover the root of our anger, we can be confident that God is with us, and He offers us all the grace and help we need.

"Let us then approach God's throne of grace with confidence, so that we may receive mercy and find grace to help us in our time of need."

HEBREWS 4:16

Write from the Heart

What other emotions typically accompany your anger? Fear, humiliation, sadness, rejection, frustration, disrespect? Explain. The answer may reveal one of the sources of your anger.

The Four Sources of Anger

Anger is typically started and fueled by at least one of four sources:

1. **Hurt**

2. **Injustice**

3. **Fear**

4. **Frustration**

Therefore, anger is a *secondary* response to one or more of these four roots.

1. Hurt: Your heart is wounded.[10]

Everyone has a God-given inner need for *unconditional love.*[11] When you experience rejection or emotional pain, anger can become a protective wall keeping people and pain away.

- **Biblical Example: The Sons of Jacob**

  Joseph was the undisputed favorite among Jacob's sons. Feeling hurt and rejected by their father, the ten older sons became angry and vindictive toward their younger brother.

  "Israel [Jacob] loved Joseph more than any of his other sons, because he had been born to him in his old age; and he made an ornate robe for him. When his brothers saw that their father loved him more than any of them, they hated him and could not speak a kind word to him" (Genesis 37:3–4).

2. Injustice: Your right is violated.[12]

Everyone has knowledge of right and wrong, fair and unfair, just and *unjust*. When you perceive an *injustice* has occurred to you or to others (especially to those you love), you may feel angry. If you hold on to the offense, the unresolved anger can begin to take root in your heart.

- **Biblical Example: Jonathan**

    King Saul's unjust treatment of David evoked Jonathan's anger. Jonathan, son of Saul, heard his own father pronounce a death sentence on his dear friend David.

    "'Why should he be put to death? What has he done?' Jonathan asked his father. But Saul hurled his spear at him to kill him [Jonathan]. Then Jonathan knew that his father intended to kill David. Jonathan got up from the table in fierce anger" (1 Samuel 20:32–34).

3. Fear: Your future is threatened.[13]

Everyone is created with a God-given inner need for *security*.[14] When you begin to worry, feel threatened, or get angry because of a change in circumstances, you may be responding to fear. A fearful heart can reveal a lack of trust in God's perfect plan for your life.

- **Biblical Example: King Saul**

    Saul became angry because of David's many successes on the battlefield. (Read 1 Samuel 18:5–15, 28–29.) He was threatened by David's popularity and feared he would lose his kingdom.

    "Saul was very angry . . . 'They have credited David with tens of thousands,' he thought, 'but me with only thousands.' . . . Saul was afraid of David, because the LORD was with David but had departed from Saul" (1 Samuel 18:8, 12).

4. Frustration: Your performance is not accepted.[15]

Everyone has a God-given inner need for *significance*.[16] When your efforts are thwarted or do not meet your own personal expectations, your sense of significance can be threatened. Frustration over unmet expectations of yourself or of others is often a major source of anger.

- **Biblical Example: Cain**

  Both Cain and Abel brought offerings to God, but Cain's offering was unacceptable. Cain chose to offer what he wanted to give rather than what God said was right and acceptable. When Cain's self-effort was rejected, his frustration led to anger, and his anger led him to murder his own brother.

  "In the course of time Cain brought some of the fruits of the soil as an offering to the LORD. And Abel also brought an offering—fat portions from some of the firstborn of his flock. The LORD looked with favor on Abel and his offering, but on Cain and his offering he did not look with favor. So Cain was very angry, and his face was downcast. . . . Now Cain said to his brother Abel, 'Let's go out to the field.' While they were in the field, Cain attacked his brother Abel and killed him" (Genesis 4:3–5, 8).

Write from the Heart

Anger has four main sources: hurt, injustice, fear, and frustration. Which of these most resonate with you and your experiences of anger? How so?

Unrealistic Expectations

Unrealistic expectations can easily lead to anger. When your expectations aren't met, the fumes of anger flame into rage. If you find yourself reacting out of anger when other people don't live up to what you expect, it may be time to adjust your expectations.

Ask yourself: "What expectations do I have toward circumstances in my life, other people, myself, and even God? Are my expectations realistic or unrealistic?"

Does this sound like you?

- "I expect my life to be just like I imagine it should be."

- "I expect people in my life to meet the benchmarks that I set for them."

- "I expect myself to live up to a standard of near perfection."

- "I expect God to grant me all that I ask of Him in prayer."

Having unrealistic expectations is like trying to put out a fire with gasoline. It only makes things worse.

- The more you expect God and people to do what you want, the angrier you become when your expectations are not met.

- The more you try to control others, the more control you give them over yourself.

- The more demands you put on others, the more power you give them to anger you.

The primary problem with unrealistic expectations is *pride*. You would be wise to ask the Lord, "Do I act as though I am the center of the world and everything revolves around me?" You need to humble yourself and submit to God and His sovereign hand over your life and over the lives of others. The Bible says the Lord's purpose prevails over our plans, so we need to leave our desires and our destiny in His hands, where they rightly belong.

> *"Many are the plans in a person's heart,*
> *but it is the LORD's purpose that prevails."*
>
> PROVERBS 19:21

Everyone has a God-given need for love, security, and significance.

Write from the Heart

What connection do you see between your anger and your expectations of yourself and others? Are unrealistic expectations a major cause of anger for you? What expectations do you need to adjust?

A Wrong "Right" to Be Angry

Prolonged anger is typically based on a *wrong* premise about *rights*. When we feel that our real or perceived rights have been violated, we can easily respond with anger.[17] And in turn, we may come to believe that we have a right to hold on to that anger for as long as we choose.

A person with prolonged anger might say . . .

- "I have had many disappointments in life, so I have a *right* to hold on to my bitterness about them."

- "Circumstances in my life are not how I want them to be, so I have a *right* to be angry about them until things get better."

- "An injustice has been done to me, so I have a *right* to retaliate in whatever way I choose."

Remember what the Bible says about suffering and trials . . .

"Now for a little while you may have had to suffer grief in all kinds of trials. These have come so that the proven genuineness of your faith—of greater worth than gold, which perishes even though refined by fire—may result in praise, glory and honor when Jesus Christ is revealed."

1 PETER 1:6–7

Wrong Belief	Right Belief
"When I feel hurt, fearful, frustrated, or have been treated unfairly, I have the right to be angry until the situation changes. It is only natural for me to be angry about the disappointments in my life and to express my anger any way I choose."	"Since I have trusted Christ with my life and have yielded my rights to Him, I choose not to be controlled by anger. My human disappointments are now God's appointments to increase my faith and develop His character in me."

Pray . . .

"Lord, thank You for being sovereign over my life. Whatever it takes, I want to respond to You with a heart of gratitude and to accept the circumstances in my life that I cannot change.

I choose to stop making myself and those around me miserable by being angry over something none of us can change.

Instead, I thank You for what You are going to teach me through this. And thank You for Your promise that somehow You are going to use this for good. In Your holy name I pray, Amen."

Discussion/Application Questions

1. Culture can have a profound impact on how we live, even if it is contrary to biblical teaching. What are the differences between what the culture says about handling anger and what the Bible says about handling anger?

   ....

   ....

   ....

   ....

   ....

   ....

2. What we learn as children often carries over into adulthood. How did your parents or other authority figures handle their anger? What did they teach you—directly or indirectly—about managing and expressing anger?

   ....

   ....

   ....

   ....

   ....

   ....

3. Read Mark 3:1–6. Why was Jesus angry with the Jewish religious leaders? What emotion accompanied His anger (v. 5)? What did He do with His anger, and what did He not do? What can you learn about handling anger from His example?

4. What is one habit that you need to begin, change, or stop to help you handle your anger more appropriately?

Notes

"Now may the Lord of peace himself give you
peace at all times and in every way."
2 Thessalonians 3:16

BIBLICAL STEPS TO SOLUTION
PART 1

*"But now you must also rid yourselves
of all such things as these:
anger, rage, malice, slander, and
filthy language from your lips."*

Colossians 3:8

Frustration Ignites Anger

On a hot, dry day, Moses' frustration reached a boiling point. He led more than a million of his people through the vast, scorching desert. But for all of his efforts, they continually complained, criticizing his leadership and condemning him for their plight: "If only we had died when our brothers fell dead! . . . Why did you bring us up out of Egypt to this terrible place?" (Numbers 20:3, 5).

Now, once again, they had no water. Earlier in their journey, God miraculously provided water by instructing Moses to strike a particular rock with his staff. When Moses obeyed, a stream of water—enough for all of Israel—poured out of the rock (Exodus 17:1–6).

At this point, God intended to perform a similar miracle. He told Moses to speak to—not strike—a certain rock. But Moses was so frustrated with the people that rather than speak to the rock, he forcefully struck the rock—not once, but twice. Gushing water is what God intended— not gushing anger. As a result, God disciplined Moses by not allowing him to lead Israel into the Promised Land (see Numbers 20:1–12).

"The LORD said to Moses and Aaron,
'Because you did not trust in me enough
to honor me as holy in the sight of the Israelites,
you will not bring this community
into the land I give them.'"

NUMBERS 20:12

At times, are you like Moses? Do you ever allow injustice, hurt, fear, or frustration to make you furious, for which you receive a painful repercussion? If so, what should you do when you become angry?

The Bible says . . .

> *"Refrain from anger and turn from wrath;*
> *do not fret—it leads only to evil."*
>
> PSALM 37:8

In this session, we'll look at how to analyze our anger and how to resolve past anger.

How to Analyze Your Anger[18]

Fire investigators are responsible for analyzing the aftermath of a fire to determine where the fire started, what started it, and why it burned out of control. The goal is to formulate a plan to prevent future fires from starting and to control and extinguish them if they break out again. Likewise, analyzing your anger will help you determine where it started, what started it, and why it got out of control, as well as how to prevent it and how to control it should it break out again.

When you honestly analyze your anger, you take the first step toward controlling your anger rather than letting your anger control you. As you practice patience and gain understanding, you will be able to use your anger for God's purposes. This will prevent foolish displays of anger you will later regret.

The following questions will help you analyze your anger. The questions are divided into two sets.

- *Question Set #1.* Use the first set of questions to help you analyze and address your anger the moment it arises.

- *Question Set #2.* Use the second set of questions to help you analyze and address your ongoing anger patterns. These questions will require more time to answer.

You can come back to the second set of questions at a later time. For now, think of a situation that recently angered you and work through the first set of questions, honestly answering each question. This will help you know how to work through the questions the next time you become angry.

Question Set #1

1. What triggered your anger?

....

....

2. What did you want?

....

....

3. How did you want to express your anger?

....

....

4. What was the result of expressing your anger?

....

....

5. Did expressing your anger help you achieve your desired outcome?

....

....

6. Were you able to calm your anger? If so, what steps did you take?

....

....

7. What can you pray about the situation and your anger right now?

....

....

Question Set #2

1. What typically triggers your anger?

....

....

2. How do you generally express your anger?

....

....

3. What do you desire when you are angry?

....

....

4. Is the way you express your anger working for you? Do you get what you desire?

5. Do you ever lose control of your anger? If so, when was the last time you did? What happened?

6. Are you able to calm your anger? If so, what do you do?

7. Have you allowed your anger to escalate? If so, what happened?

8. Is your anger harming your relationships? If so, how?

9. Has your anger ever caused any health problems? If so, what?

....

....

10. Do others point out your anger even if you don't see it? If so, when and what do they say?

....

....

11. Does your anger ever become physical? If so, how and how often?

....

....

12. When you get angry, how safe do you feel?

....

....

13. When you get angry, how safe do others feel?

....

....

....

14. Did anyone in your childhood home have an anger problem? If so, who, and how were you impacted back then?

....

....

15. As a child, how did you feel when you were on the receiving end of someone's anger?

....

....

16. Do you think anger from your childhood is still impacting you today? If so, how?

....

....

17. Do you have difficulty forgiving those toward whom you have anger? If so, explain.

....

....

18. Is there someone wise you can talk to about your anger?

....

....

19. Do you ever pray about your anger? If so, what do you pray?

....

....

20. What is your view of God when you are experiencing anger?

....

....

21. How do you think you should respond to God when you feel angry?

....

....

22. How do you think you should respond to others when you feel angry?

....

....

23. What can you learn from a recent anger problem that will help you better handle your anger in the future?

....

....

....

How to Resolve Your Past Anger

Have you ever seen a picture of someone walking on hot coals? They appear to defy nature by taking a short, yet potentially scorching, journey with feet unscathed. It's no mystery that the trick to salvaging the soles is to move fast, never lingering long enough for the fiery coals to begin burning the skin. If for some reason the treacherous trek is prolonged, pain and injury will ensue.

Failure to resolve past anger operates in much the same way. The longer it resides in your heart, the more painful and injurious it is for you and for others. That's because unresolved anger produces bitterness. And bitterness is like a bed of hidden coals burning deep wounds into your heart. It can damage your relationships and snatch joy from your heart and peace from your spirit.

"Get rid of all bitterness, rage and anger, brawling and slander, along with every form of malice. Be kind and compassionate to one another, forgiving each other, just as in Christ God forgave you."

EPHESIANS 4:31–32

The following eight steps will help you put away past anger.

1. Realize your unresolved anger.

- **Admit** you have harbored anger in your heart and confess it as sin.

- **Ask** God to reveal all of your unresolved anger.

- **Admit** to a wise, nonjudgmental friend or counselor that you have buried anger.

- **Ask** God to help you see your sin as He sees your sin.

Say to the Lord, "I confess my iniquity; I am troubled by my sin" (Psalm 38:18).

2. Revisit your root feelings.

- **Did you feel hurt:** rejected, betrayed, unloved, ignored?

- **Did you experience injustice:** cheated, wronged, maligned, attacked?

- **Did you feel fearful:** threatened, insecure, out-of-control, powerless?

- **Did you feel frustrated:** inadequate, inferior, hindered, controlled?

Pray to the Lord, "Search me, God, and know my heart; test me and know my anxious thoughts. See if there is any offensive way in me, and lead me in the way everlasting" (Psalm 139:23–24).

3. Release your "rights" regarding the offense.

- **Release** your right to hear "I'm sorry" for the offense.

- **Release** your right to dwell on the offense.

- **Release** your right to hold on to the offense.

- **Release** your right to keep bringing up the offense.

Remember, "Whoever would foster love covers over an offense, but whoever repeats the matter separates close friends" (Proverbs 17:9).

4. Recognize your need to forgive.

- **Make** a list of each of your hurts. Release each one to God. Then dispose of the list.

- **Pray** that the Lord will heal whatever is broken in those who mistreat you.

- **Give** your desire for revenge to God. Do not strike back or retaliate.

- **Release** those who have hurt you into the hands of God. Forgive as God forgave you!

Be faithful to "bear with each other and forgive one another if any of you has a grievance against someone. Forgive as the Lord forgave you" (Colossians 3:13).

5. Rejoice in God's purpose for allowing your pain.

- **Thank God** for the ways He will use this trial in your life for your good.

- **Thank God** for how He will use your resolved anger for the good of others.

- **Thank God** for His promise to restore you after a time of suffering.

- **Thank God** for His promise to use all the pain to make you strong, firm, and steadfast.

Give thanks that "the God of all grace, who called you to his eternal glory in Christ, after you have suffered a little while, will himself restore you and make you strong, firm and steadfast" (1 Peter 5:10).

6. Restore the relationship when appropriate.

- **Confess your anger** both to God and to the person with whom you have resisted reconciliation.

- **Keep the encounter** free of anger and accusatory statements.

- **State your desire** for reconciliation within a right relationship.

(Please remember that sometimes reconciliation may not be appropriate, such as with an abuser or between people involved in an adulterous affair or other destructive relationships. Talk with a trusted pastor or counselor who can help you to determine if reconciliation is advisable in your situation; and if so, how you can go about reconciling safely with appropriate boundaries.)

Remember Jesus' words: "I tell you that anyone who is angry with a brother or sister will be subject to judgment. . . . Therefore, if you are offering your gift at the altar and there remember that your brother or sister has something against you, leave your gift there in front of the altar. First go and be reconciled to them; then come and offer your gift" (Matthew 5:22–24).

7. Receive God's love for you personally.

- **Personalize** Bible verses that reveal God's love for you: Jeremiah 31:3; Lamentations 3:22–23; Ephesians 2:4–5.

- **Read** these Scriptures daily until you can recite them: Psalm 32:10; 89:1; 103:17.

- **Rely** on the Lord to meet your inner needs for love, significance, and security.[19]

- **Thank God** each day for His unconditional love (1 John 3:1).

Pray like the apostle Paul: "That you, being rooted and established in love, may have power, together with all the Lord's holy people, to grasp how wide and long and high and deep is the love of Christ, and to know this love that surpasses knowledge—that you may be filled to the measure of all the fullness of God" (Ephesians 3:17–19).

8. Reflect Christ's love.

- **Reflect the love of Jesus by praying** for every person who hurts or angers you.

"Lord, may **my heart** be a reflection of Your heart."

"Lord, may **my mind** be an expression of Your mind."

"Lord, may **my will** be an illustration of Your will."

"Lord, may **my love** be a demonstration of Your love."

Jesus said, "A new command I give you: Love one another. As I have loved you, so you must love one another. By this everyone will know that you are my disciples, if you love one another" (John 13:34–35).

Pray for every person who hurts or angers you.

Write from the Heart

Which of the eight steps for resolving past anger seems to be the most difficult for you to do? Why?

....

....

....

....

....

Take a moment to write a prayer, asking God to help put away past anger.

....

....

....

....

....

....

Discussion/Application Questions

1. Read Matthew 5:21–26. What does Jesus say about anger in this passage (vv. 21–22)? What is His solution to resolving anger (vv. 23–26)?

....

....

....

....

2. How does anger affect your relationships (with your spouse, children, parents, friends, co-workers, etc.)? Is there someone you need to forgive for their anger, or that you need to ask forgiveness for displaying inappropriate anger?

....

....

....

....

3. Does your anger typically control you or do you control your anger? What seems to be the biggest barrier that prevents you from managing anger in a healthy, godly way?

....

....

. . . .

. . . .

. . . .

. . . .

4. Read Ephesians 4:26. If you applied this verse every day, what would the impact be on your life and your relationships?

. . . .

. . . .

. . . .

. . . .

. . . .

5. Read Psalm 103:8–12. What does this passage say about God's anger? Even though we sin, what does this passage say about how God treats us? Write out a prayer, thanking God for not treating you in anger—as your sins deserve—but treating you with grace.

. . . .

. . . .

. . . .

. . . .

. . . .

Notes

"Now may the Lord of peace himself give you
peace at all times and in every way."
2 Thessalonians 3:16

SESSION 5

BIBLICAL STEPS TO SOLUTION
PART 2

*"When I am in distress, I call to you,
because you answer me."*

PSALM 86:7

An Opportunity to Trust

Have you ever blamed God for the pain and heartache in your life? Have you ever pointed a condemning finger because He has not stopped evil and suffering?

In the Bible, a man named Job seriously questioned God—so much so that we can hear anger in his bitter complaint: "Even today my complaint is bitter; his [God's] hand is heavy in spite of my groaning. If only I knew where to find him; if only I could go to his dwelling! I would state my case before him and fill my mouth with arguments" (Job 23:2–4).

But is anger toward God justifiable? While He understands our anger, notice how He answers Job: "Who is this that obscures my plans with words without knowledge? . . . Will the one who contends with the Almighty correct him?" (Job 38:2; 40:2).

God asks Job a series of questions about creation and the natural world, "Where were you when I laid the earth's foundation? Tell me, if you understand. . . . Have you comprehended the vast expanses of the earth? Tell me, if you know all this" (Job 38:4, 18). The point of these questions is to show Job that he is finite. He is limited in his perspective, knowledge, and understanding. When Job later repents, he says, "Surely I spoke of things I did not understand, things too wonderful for me to know" (Job 42:3).

Like Job, we are all finite and limited. We often fail to see how God is using our trials and suffering for good. Instead of running to God, we run away from God or shake our fist at God. But God is not surprised by our anger or other difficult emotions. He wants us to come to Him, no matter what we're dealing with and no matter what we are feeling. When we are angry, it is an opportunity to trust God and pour our hearts out to Him.

> *"Trust in him at all times, you people;*
> *pour out your hearts to him,*
> *for God is our refuge."*
>
> PSALM 62:8

In this session, we'll look at how to resolve our anger toward God and how God can use our anger for His purposes.

How to Resolve Your Anger toward God

What is the answer to intense anger against God? Can it be resolved? And if so, how? The sure way to resolve your anger toward God is to gain a full understanding of the character, purpose, and plan of God.

1. Know God's Character.

- **He is just.**

  "He is the Rock, his works are perfect, and all his ways are just. A faithful God who does no wrong, upright and just is he" (Deuteronomy 32:4).

- **His ways are just.**

  "Just and true are your ways, King of the nations" (Revelation 15:3).

- **He is love.**

  "God is love" (1 John 4:8).

- **He loves us.**

  "We love because he first loved us" (1 John 4:19).

2. Know God's Purposes.

- **He brings good out of evil.**

  "We know that in all things God works for the good of those who love him" (Romans 8:28).

- **He turns your sorrow into joy.**

  "You turned my wailing into dancing; you removed my sackcloth and clothed me with joy" (Psalm 30:11).

- **He uses your suffering to produce perseverance, character, and hope.**

  "We also glory in our sufferings, because we know that suffering produces perseverance; perseverance, character; and character, hope. And hope does not put us to shame, because God's love has been poured out into our hearts through the Holy Spirit, who has been given to us" (Romans 5:3–5).

- **He uses your troubles to teach you compassion.**

  "The Father of compassion and the God of all comfort . . . comforts us in all our troubles, so that we can comfort those in any trouble with the comfort we ourselves receive from God" (2 Corinthians 1:3–4).

3. Know God's Plan.

- **He will grant eternal life to you and all who entrust their lives to Christ.**

  "My Father's will is that everyone who looks to the Son and believes in him shall have eternal life, and I will raise them up at the last day" (John 6:40).

- **He will bless you if you persevere under trial.**

  "Blessed is the one who perseveres under trial" (James 1:12).

- **He will bring His righteous judgment on those who are evil.**

  "The Lord knows how to rescue the godly from trials and to hold the unrighteous for punishment on the day of judgment" (2 Peter 2:9).

- **He will, one day, make everything new for His people.**

  "I heard a loud voice from the throne saying, 'Look! God's dwelling place is now among the people, and he will dwell with them. They will be his people, and God himself will be with them and be their God. "He will wipe every tear from their eyes. There will be no more death" or mourning or crying or pain, for the old order of things has passed away.' He who was seated on the throne said, 'I am making everything new!'" (Revelation 21:3–5).

Job, who at one time had anger toward God, ultimately realized that he had misplaced anger. With deepest remorse, he admitted his wrong.

"I know that you can do all things;
no purpose of yours can be thwarted. . . .
My ears had heard of you
but now my eyes have seen you.
Therefore I despise myself
and repent in dust and ashes."

JOB 42:2, 5–6

Write from the Heart

Look over the section about knowing God's character, purposes, and plan again. Choose the points or Bible passages that are particularly meaningful to you, as it relates to your anger. How does knowing about God's character, plan, and purposes change the way you understand and handle your anger?

A Question about Evil

Many of us get angry at God for allowing bad people to cause so much pain. The question often asked is: "Since God had the power to create the world, why doesn't He stop evil in the world?"

God allows evil because He allows people to exercise free will. He did not create us to be robots with no choice to do anything except what the Creator has programmed. He created us to be "free agent" human beings who have a choice over what we think, say, and do. We can't have it both ways, in that God allows us freedom but we can't do anything wrong. That's not freedom!

If you have read Revelation 20:11–21:5, you know that God has appointed a time in the future when He will put an end to evil and suffering.

The bad news is that until then, evil will always be in opposition to good, and it will be a struggle to live in a fallen world.

But the good news is that God is with us in our pain and can use harmful experiences to accomplish His purposes. He did so in the life of Joseph, whose brothers sold him into slavery. Years later, the frightened brothers came face-to-face with him. By then, Joseph was the prime minister of Egypt and had saved both the Egyptians and the Hebrews from famine. Joseph said to his brothers . . .

"Don't be afraid. Am I in the place of God?
You intended to harm me,
but God intended it for good
to accomplish what is now being done,
the saving of many lives."

GENESIS 50:19–20

How to Accept God's Aim for Anger

Forest rangers who care for and protect national parks occasionally say they have to "start a fire to stop a fire." Known as *backfires*, these fires help deprive the main fire of fuel and better enable forest rangers and firefighters to contain the blaze. At times, God works for your good in much the same way.

God intends for you to experience the emotion of anger and to use it for some positive purpose. For example, He can use your anger to spark your awareness of a blazing spiritual problem that needs to be snuffed out. God often allows fiery trials to test your faith and to develop the perseverance necessary to sustain your faith.

> *"Consider it pure joy, my brothers and sisters, whenever you face trials of many kinds, because you know that the testing of your faith produces perseverance."*
>
> JAMES 1:2–3

As you seek to allow God to direct your anger and use it for His purposes, remember . . .

- **Anger** can bring your true feelings to light.

- **Anger** can uncover your need to set healthy boundaries.

- **Anger** can be used to bring positive change in your life.

- **Anger** can help you gain insight into past hurts.

- **Anger** can be the spark that encourages healthy, appropriate, honest communication in relationships.

- **Anger** can be used by God, when expressed appropriately, to convict others of sin.

- **Anger** can reveal your inappropriate ways of trying to meet your own needs.

- **Anger** can be used by God to motivate others to make responsible decisions.

- **Anger** can help you realize your need for the Lord.

Remember, anger is not inherently sinful. God can use it for good purposes. By His grace, it is possible to not sin in your anger.

"'In your anger do not sin':
Do not let the sun go down
while you are still angry."

EPHESIANS 4:26

Allow God to direct your anger
and use it for His purposes.

Write from the Heart

The analogy of fire has been used throughout this study to give you a clear picture of anger. Like fire, what are some destructive characteristics of anger? What positive outcomes can anger produce?

Discussion/Application Questions

1. Name a Bible character or someone from your life who handled anger in a godly way. What did they do? What did they *not* do? What can you learn from their example?

2. Describe how God used something that angered you to accomplish His good purposes. What did you learn from that experience?

3. Read Romans 12:17–21. How does this passage apply to managing anger? What would it look like to apply this passage to a current situation in your life?

....

....

....

....

....

....

....

4. Read Luke 6:28. What can you pray for those who have angered you? Take a moment and write out a prayer for anyone who has been a source of anger for you.

....

....

....

....

....

....

....

Notes

"Now may the Lord of peace himself give you
peace at all times and in every way."
2 Thessalonians 3:16

Biblical Steps to Solution
PART 3

"[Love] is not easily angered."

1 CORINTHIANS 13:5

The Quick Answer to Anger

Members of a First Response Team know the importance of having a *quick answer*. In the face of calamity, firefighters must provide a quick response but remain cool under pressure. When you sense a surge of anger, it's vital that you learn to respond quickly. If not, your anger could blaze out of control.

The possibility of out-of-control anger remains ever present. A spark of irritation can be ignited intentionally by hurtful people or even unintentionally by those who love you. God wants you to seek His answer for anger quickly before it burns the bridges of your relationships because "human anger does not produce the righteousness that God desires" (James 1:20).

If we had to boil down all efforts to manage anger to the most basic steps, the solution could be reduced to two points: one question and one action step.

> **Step 1. Ask** – Can I change this situation?

> **Step 2. Action** – If you can, change it.
> If you can't, release it.

Let's go back to the first step: Can you change what angers you? Answer *yes* or *no*—that's it.

Now consider the second step: If you answered *yes*, you are angry about something you can change—so change it.

> **If the door squeaks**, oil it.
> **If the faucet leaks**, fix it.

If you answered *no*, you are angry about something you cannot change—so release it.

How do you release your anger? First, list what angers you—every person, every situation. Then, humbly go to God, refusing to demand your rights, rejecting any thought of revenge, and surrendering the situation and yourself to the Lord—past, present, and future. Although you may feel completely powerless, the truth is you have the power to release your pain and anger to Him.

"Cast all your anxiety on him because he cares for you."

1 PETER 5:7

In this session, we'll look at how to apply the quick answer to anger and look at eight practical steps on how to handle our anger.

You have the power to release your pain and anger to God.

THE TWO-STEP SOLUTION

Think of a situation in which you typically find yourself angry. Apply the two steps.

STEP 1:

Can you change it? (YES or NO)

....

STEP 2:

YES. How will you change it?

....

....

....

....

....

NO. How will you release it into God's hands?

....

....

....

....

....

How to Alleviate Your Present Anger

A firefighter's job is not done until all the flames are extinguished. Having a quick answer to anger is helpful in a variety of situations. But a more thorough plan can help fully extinguish the effects of anger in your life. Like a firefighter's hose spraying water on a fire, working through the following eight A's can do much to douse the potentially dangerous effects of anger in your life.

1. Acknowledge Your Anger.

- **Be willing** to admit you have anger.

- **Be aware** of when you feel angry.

- **Become aware** of how you suppress your anger either because of fear or pride.

- **Be willing** to take responsibility for any inappropriate anger.

Realize, "Whoever conceals their sins does not prosper, but the one who confesses and renounces them finds mercy" (Proverbs 28:13).

2. Ascertain Your Style.

- **How often** do you feel angry? Often? Sometimes? Seldom? Never?

- **How do you know** when you are angry?

- **How do others know** when you are angry?

- **How do you release** your anger? Do you explode? Do you criticize? Do you joke or tease? Do you become sarcastic, defensive, or teary-eyed?

Pray, "Test me, LORD, and try me, examine my heart and my mind" (Psalm 26:2).

3. Assess the Source.

- **Hurt.** Is the source of your anger hurt feelings from the words or actions of others?

- **Injustice.** Is the source of your anger the unjust actions of someone toward you or another person?

- **Fear.** Is the source of your anger fear because of a recent or anticipated loss?

- **Frustration.** Is the source of your anger frustration over blocked plans, hopes, or dreams?

Commit to total honesty before God. "I know, my God, that you test the heart and are pleased with integrity" (1 Chronicles 29:17).

4. Appraise Your Thinking.

- **Are you expecting** others to meet your standards?

- **Are you guilty** of distorted thinking (assuming, exaggerating, generalizing, labeling, etc.)?

- **Are you believing lies** about God or about yourself?

- **Are you blaming** God or others?

Remember, "The wicked put up a bold front, but the upright give thought to their ways" (Proverbs 21:29).

Write from the Heart

Do #4 (Appraise Your Thinking) right now. This exercise will help you identify truth when you're angry. What negative thought do you often repeat in your mind? Write it down.

....

....

....

....

....

Next, write down a Bible passage or scriptural truth that speaks directly to that negative thought.

....

....

....

....

....

....

....

5. Admit Your Needs.

- **Do you use manipulative anger** as a ploy in an attempt to feel loved?

- **Do you use explosive anger**, insisting on certain conditions in order to feel significant?

- **Do you use controlling anger** to demand your way in order to feel secure?

- **Do you know** that only Christ can ultimately meet all of your inner needs for love, significance, and security?

Rest assured, "My God will meet all your needs according to the riches of his glory in Christ Jesus" (Philippians 4:19).

6. Abandon Your Demands.

Instead of demanding that others meet your inner needs for love, significance, and security, learn to look to the Lord to meet your needs.[20] Look to the Lord to meet your need for . . .

- **Love**

  "Lord, though I would like to feel more love from others, I know You love me unconditionally, and you will love me forever."

  "I have loved you with an everlasting love; I have drawn you with unfailing kindness" (Jeremiah 31:3).

- **Significance**

  "Lord, though I would like to feel more significant to those around me, I know I am significant in Your eyes."

  "'I know the plans I have for you,' declares the Lord, 'plans to prosper you and not to harm you, plans to give you hope and a future'" (Jeremiah 29:11).

- **Security**

  "Lord, though I wish I felt more secure in my relationships, I know I am secure in my relationship with You."

  "The Lord is with me; I will not be afraid. What can mere mortals do to me?" (Psalm 118:6).

- **Life and godliness**

  "Lord, though I wish others would be more responsive to my needs, I know You have promised to meet all of my needs."

  "His divine power has given us everything we need for a godly life through our knowledge of him who called us by his own glory and goodness" (2 Peter 1:3).

Constantly remind yourself, "God is able to bless you abundantly, so that in all things at all times, having all that you need, you will abound in every good work" (2 Corinthians 9:8).

*Look to the Lord
to meet your needs.*

7. Address Your Anger.

Determine whether your anger is really justified.

- Has a wrong been committed?

- Has anyone suffered hurt or injury?

- Has an injustice occurred?

Consider, "This is what the LORD Almighty says: 'Give careful thought to your ways'" (Haggai 1:5).

Decide on the appropriate response.

- How important is the issue?

- Would a good purpose be served if I mention it?

- Should I acknowledge my anger only to the Lord?

Remember, "[There is] a time to be silent and a time to speak" (Ecclesiastes 3:7).

Depend on the Holy Spirit for guidance.

- Ask for counsel about your anger.

- Ask for insight about your anger.

- Ask for wisdom about your anger.

Be assured that "The Spirit of truth . . . will guide you into all the truth. . . . and he will tell you what is yet to come" (John 16:13).

Develop constructive dialogue if you need to confront an offender.

- Don't speak rashly with a heart of unforgiveness. Think carefully before you speak.

- Don't use "you" phrases such as: "How could you . . . ?" or "Why can't you . . . ?" Use personal statements such as "I feel . . ." or "I need . . ."

- Don't bring up past grievances. Stay focused on the present issue.

- Don't assume the other person is wrong. Listen for feedback from another point of view.

- Don't expect instant understanding. Be patient and respond with a gentle tone of voice.

Remember, "A gentle answer turns away wrath, but a harsh word stirs up anger" (Proverbs 15:1).

8. Alter Your Attitudes.

Read Philippians 2:2–8.

- Have the goal to be like-minded with Christ.

  "Make my joy complete by being like-minded, having the same love, being one in spirit and of one mind" (v. 2).

- Do not think of yourself first.

  "Do nothing out of selfish ambition or vain conceit" (v. 3).

- Give the other person preferential treatment.

  "Rather, in humility value others above yourselves . . ." (v. 3).

- Consider the interests of the other person.

  "Not looking to your own interests but each of you to the interests of the others" (v. 4).

- Have the attitude of Jesus Christ.

  "In your relationships with one another, have the same mindset as Christ Jesus . . . " (v. 5).

- Do not emphasize your position or rights.

  "Who, being in very nature God, did not consider equality with God something to be used to his own advantage . . . " (v. 6).

- Look for ways to serve others.

  " . . . rather, he made himself nothing by taking the very nature of a servant, being made in human likeness" (v. 7).

- Speak and act with a humble spirit.

  "And being found in appearance as a man, he humbled himself . . . " (v. 8).

- Obey the Word of God, and submit your will to His will.

  " . . . by becoming obedient . . . " (v. 8).

- Be willing to die to your own desires.

  " . . . to death—even death on a cross!" (v. 8).

When you feel angry about an issue, if you can, change it—if you can't, release it. Release it into the hands of your sovereign Savior!

Write from the Heart

Read Philippians 2:2–8 again. With respect to anger, what do you learn here about Christ's selfless example of service? What does this reveal to you about how you should handle anger?

Discussion/Application Questions

1. How has your understanding of anger changed over the past six sessions? What are one or two key takeaways the Lord has revealed to you about anger? How will that impact your life and how you handle anger?

2. As you look ahead, describe at least one habit in your life that will begin, change, or stop in order to help you handle your anger in a more Christlike way.

3. Who in your life struggles with anger? What truths from this study would be helpful for them to know? What steps can you take to become a listening ear for them—to give them a safe place to talk about their anger?

....

....

....

....

....

....

4. Read Psalm 68:19. As we conclude this study, spend a moment praising and thanking God for bearing your burdens, guiding you, and helping you address your anger. Write down all the reasons for which you can thank God.

....

....

....

....

....

....

....

....

Notes

"*Now may the Lord of peace himself give you
peace at all times and in every way.*"
2 Thessalonians 3:16

Endnotes

1. Ray Burwick, *The Menace Within: Hurt or Anger?* (Birmingham, AL: Ray Burwick, 1985), 18; Gary D. Chapman, *The Other Side of Love: Handling Anger in a Godly Way* (Chicago: Moody, 1999), 17–18.

2. W. E. Vine, et al., *Vine's Complete Expository Dictionary of Biblical Words*, electronic ed. (Nashville: Thomas Nelson, 1996), s.v. "nose."

3. Ibid., s.v. "anger, angry."

4. David R. Mace, *Love & Anger in Marriage* (Grand Rapids: Zondervan, 1982), 42–45.

5. James Mahoney, *Dealing with Anger* (Dallas: Rapha, n.d.), audiocassette; H. Norman Wright, *Anger* (Waco, TX: Word, 1980), audiocassette.

6. Scholastic, "Career as a Volcanologist," an interview with Dr. Stanley Williams, http://www2.scholastic.com/browse/article.jsp?id=4877.

7. Ray Burwick, *The Menace Within: Hurt or Anger?* (Birmingham, AL: Ray Burwick, 1985), 33–50.

8. Les Carter, *Getting the Best of Your Anger* (Dallas: Rapha, n.d.), audiocassette; Wright, *Anger*, audiocassette.

9. Michael Milstein, "Scientists Continue to Learn From Mount St. Helens," *The Oregonian* (January, 29, 2009).

10. Wright, *Anger*, audiocassette.

11. Lawrence J. Crabb, Jr., *Understanding People: Deep Longings for Relationship*, Ministry Resources Library (Grand Rapids: Zondervan, 1987), 15–16; Robert S. McGee, *The Search for Significance*, 2nd ed. (Houston, TX: Rapha, 1990), 27–30.

12. Gary Jackson Oliver and H. Norman Wright, *When Anger Hits Home* (Chicago: Moody, 1992), 97.

13. Wright, *Anger*, audiocassette.

14. McGee, *The Search for Significance*, 27; Crabb, *Understanding People*, 15–16.

15. Wright, *Anger*, audiocassette.

16. McGee, *The Search for Significance*, 27; Crabb, *Understanding People*, 15–16.

17. Gary D. Chapman, *The Other Side of Love: Handling Anger in a Godly Way* (Chicago: Moody, 1999), 21; Russell Kelfer, *Tough Choices* (San Antonio, TX: Into His Likeness, 1991), 59–60, 65.

18. David Powlison, "Anger Part 2: Three Lies About Anger and the Transforming Truth," *The Journal of Biblical Counseling* 14, no. 2 (Winter 1996): 18–21.

19. McGee, *The Search for Significance*, 27–30; Crabb, *Understanding People*, 15–16.

20. McGee, *The Search for Significance*, 27–30; Crabb, *Understanding People*, 15–16.

HOPE FOR THE HEART
Biblically Based Studies on Everyday Issues
6-Session Bible Studies

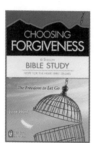

CHOOSING FORGIVENESS
Learn how you can be an expression of God's grace by forgiving others and find the freedom He intended you to have.
ISBN: 9781628623840

DEALING WITH ANGER
Have you ever reacted rashly out of anger—and lived to regret it? You can learn to keep your anger under control and learn how to act rather than react.
ISBN: 9781628623871

OVERCOMING DEPRESSION
Can anything dispel the darkness of depression? The answer is yes! Let God lead you through the storm and into the light.
ISBN: 9781628623901

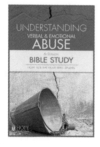

UNDERSTANDING VERBAL AND EMOTIONAL ABUSE
You can learn biblical truths and practical "how to's" for stopping the pain of abuse and for restoring peace in all your relationships.
ISBN: 9781628623932

HANDLING STRESS
Discover biblical approaches to handling stress. God wants to be your source of calm in stressful situations.
ISBN: 9781628623963

FINDING SELF-WORTH IN CHRIST
Learn to leave behind feelings of worthlessness, and experience the worth you have in the eyes of your heavenly Father.
ISBN: 9781628623994